Processions
of God

Processions
of God

THE SIGNIFICANCE OF CEREMONY

REVISED AND ENLARGED EDITION

J. E. Leonard

LAUDEMONT PRESS

CHICAGO

They have seen Thy procession, O God,
The procession of my God, my King,
into the sanctuary.

Psalm 68:24

Contents

Introduction

Throughout the history of the world there have been many distinctive cultures which rise and fall like the tide, dominating the society of humankind for a brief moment and then fading into oblivion, leaving a froth of foam behind them as a reminder. Historians have titles for these periods, names like "the Enlightenment," "the Victorian Era," "the Roaring Twenties." The modern world of the twentieth century has been called the Electronic Age, the Age of Relativism, the New Age, and a variety of other labels. But in light of the study we are about to undertake we shall define it as "the Casual Age."

The Casual Age is characterized by a lack of formality in all areas of life. "Be comfortable" is its watchword and "If it feels good, do it," is its motto. It is not simply that people in the Casual Age neglect proper form in the living of their lives; rather, it is that ceremony has become an accursed thing, the symbol of those restrictions and standards generally rejected and even despised by the present generation.

Columnist Robert Preston has written about his accommodation to the Casual Age and the sense of loss he has experienced as a result. Preston and his family had gone to church "on a Saturday afternoon because it was convenient." Looking around, he noticed that other parishioners were dressed as he was, in clothes more suitable to a game of golf or a trip to the amusement park than to the house of God.

He was especially aware of the children in attendance that day, and asked himself the question, "How do these youngsters distinguish between the important and the ordinary?" Musing on the answer to that question he came to the conclusion that they could not. He comments:

> There remains for me a nagging fear that something is more at issue here than just the fact that "Sunday clothes" belong to a bygone era. ...We are losing from our society the concept of the formal, and I use that term in its philosophical meaning of the "form" as that principle which gives meaning. It is through the form that we grasp what things are for.[1]

Americans in our society are largely concerned, Preston concludes, with what is convenient and not so much with what is important.

It has not always been thus. In earlier times ceremony was recognized as a necessity to every sort of relationship. Ceremony was employed to create and maintain a civilized society, to define and enhance important occasions in the life of the individual or the community, and to make sense of life's good times and bad times. Ancient peoples enacted elaborate rituals for use in making covenants with one another, harvesting crops, preparing for battle, burying the dead, worshiping the gods or whatever else was deemed noteworthy. A casual approach to such events would have been unthinkable.

In our society the disavowing of formality has become a value, and the widespread acceptance of this value has wrought a profound change in our approach to life. It goes hand in hand with an attitude of relevance, a lack of ultimate authority or standards. There is no longer a right or wrong way to do a thing. We have the idea that to engage in ceremony means we are taking things too seriously and that can be a bit embarrassing. Along with a loss of a sense of the formal, we have also lost discipline and structure.

Although such a loss diminishes all areas of our lives, it is particularly damaging when we carry a casual attitude into the sanctuary of God. Even in an earthly kingdom one does not enter the presence of an absolute monarch on his or her own terms. Yet that is what we are often guilty of attempting when we come before the Lord. That may mean that we do not take our encounter with him as seriously as we ought.

This book will examine the importance of ritual in our culture and particularly in our worship. We will look at some possible reasons for the spirit of informality which has overtaken us and come to some conclusions about what we might do to correct it. In all of this we will

---

[1]Robert A. Preston, "Sadly, 'Casual' Is a State of Mind," *Chicago Tribune,* February 20, 1995.

seek to be informed by the Word of God and enlightened by his Spirit.

1

The Functions of Ceremony

Ceremony is useful in maintaining civilization because it performs certain specific functions in the society. One of these is to *create a context for human experience*. The journey from birth to death is traversed in a series of stages, each of which begins with a significant change or an achievement which propels us into the next phase. These changes are traditionally marked by what is called a "rite of passage," an acknowledgment of some kind that a corner has been turned and life will now be different.

Experience teaches us that rites of passage in the life of an individual take on shape and structure when they occur within a formal setting. Think of weddings, for example. When a man and woman plan carefully for a meaningful ceremony and perhaps a celebration which will enact the commitment they are making to each other, it is an evidence of the seriousness with which they approach their union. Most couples are concerned to order the wedding according to customs which are familiar, those they have received from their own families and the society of which they are a part. Whether the vows are spoken at a small, at-home affair, in the judge's chambers, or as part of a full-scale, formal church extravaganza, traditional rituals build a framework which marks this event as a wedding. Even when the bride and groom decide to write their own unique vows, and even in spite of differences in cultural backgrounds and individual style, a wedding always looks, sounds and feels like a wedding.

The same is true of graduation exercises. There is a recognizable form by which such commencements are ordered. In our culture they typically involve slow, dignified processions of persons wearing a particular type of clothing or robes, with square, flat caps on their heads, who walk across a raised platform, shake hands by turns with a dignitary from the institution from which they are graduating, and are each handed a ribbon-tied scroll. The diplomas or degrees might more easily be passed out to students as they leave school on the last day of class, but that would be emotionally unsatisfying. Commencement exercises provide a structure for the culmination of the educational process at a given level, and the subsequent passing of the student into another phase of life experience.

On a less formal scale is the retirement party, given for a long-time employee who has attained the age at which he may now take advantage of the retirement program offered by his place of business. It is possible to simply leave work on one's last day and not come back, but there is a feeling of emptiness, a lack of closure when a long relationship is ended so abruptly. In order to smooth the transition for both employer and employee a social event takes place. The departing employee is praised for his or her contributions to the company and perhaps given gifts. There is feasting and fellowship and many good wishes expressed for the future.

A second function of ceremony is to *link an individual to the community*. At various times in a person's life he connects to the life of the community as a whole, and these points of contact are traditionally celebrated with formal rituals. The Jewish custom of circumcising male infants, the Christian practice of liturgical baptism, membership rites in fraternal and religious organizations, confirmations and *bar mitzvahs* and *bas mitzvahs* all demonstrate the community function of ceremony. In each of these examples the candidates go through prescribed steps which, when accomplished, culminate in membership in the society. Participating with the novitiates in the rituals are those who have themselves gone through initiation and are now established in the community. By means of the ceremonies the culture of the group is maintained and passed down to succeeding generations.

Ceremony not only connects the individual to the community; it also, thirdly, *creates a group identity*. The rites which are practiced by fraternal organizations, for example, are known only to those who have committed themselves to the brotherhood. Visitors would not understand what is taking place in a ritual of the Grange or the Eastern Star; indeed, they would not be permitted even to watch. Similarly, the Protestant who attends mass for the first time is bewildered by the standing and kneeling, the responses and songs, all done from memory by the congregation. He may even feel estranged and out of place. But this is as it should be. Ceremony is for the initiated, and it tends to collect individuals and make of them a whole.

When we allow entry into our churches to become too easy, we run the risk of removing the distinctive ethos that identifies our particular church. Such things as allowing anyone present to participate in the communion, serving the bread and cup in the pew so there is no need to know the procedure, and announcing every move the congregation is expected to make so the newcomer will "feel at home" tend to remove incentive for the outsider to become an insider. He need make no effort to penetrate the community because there are no depths to plumb. The mystery has been removed. On the other hand, to insist that anyone who wishes to become part of us must go through the initiatory rite of baptism, attend classes in order to learn the tenets to which we all subscribe, and learn to participate in private rituals which are for believers only, is to understand that such ceremonies identify us and, indeed, help to make us who we are.

Stanley Hauerwas has written about the necessity for the Christian community to maintain an "us-them" mentality in order to be authentic. Christians, he maintains, are always at war. He comments:

> One hopes that God is using this time to remind the Church that Christianity is unintelligible without enemies. Indeed, the whole point of Christianity is to produce the right kind of enemies. We have been beguiled by our established status to forget that to be a Christian is to be made part of an army against armies.[2]

If we look at the history of both Israel and the church, we will find that these communities always understood themselves as having been set in opposition to the culture around them. They were not to become entangled with that alien culture, and it was not to be assimilated into them. Perhaps the reason people are not clamoring

---

[2]Stanley Hauerwas, "Preaching As Though We Had Enemies," *First Things,* No. 53 (May, 1995), 47.

to join our churches is that in our effort to make newcomers feel comfortable we have destroyed our own distinctive identity. Forgetting that the church is a gathering of *believers* who meet to reaffirm their covenant vows with their Lord, we have tried to make it accessible to anyone who decides to walk through the doors, hoping they will like us well enough to return. This was not so in the early church, where the unbaptized were not allowed even to observe the celebration of Eucharist. Nor was it a simple matter to become one of the baptized, for the period of instruction and preparation was sometimes as long as three years.

It might be well to ask ourselves why the Mormons, or Latter Day Saints, continue to experience such remarkable growth. One major reason must be that the Mormon church maintains a strong identity through its secret ceremonies, its beautiful temples which are closed to non-members, special undergarments worn by the faithful, and the strong sense of community these things engender. Similarly, the appeal of Freemasonry and other fraternal organizations is strengthened through the rituals and activities, codes of loyalty, or secret handshakes and other symbols which are known only to members in good standing. All of these things create a sense of brotherhood among those who are selected to become members.

Perhaps the popularity of these organizations is due to the fact that they fill the void left by a church which has abandoned its own sense of separateness and is no longer distinguishable from the world. In the West, we now live in a culture which promotes the right of every person to do or experience what every other person does or experiences. But this cannot be so in the church. We must recover those sacred rituals which separate the faithful from the uninitiated if we are to retain our identity and make an impact in the midst of a secular society.

In the fourth place, ceremony serves to *confer significance upon an event.* Most people would not interrupt their daily routines or set aside their own recreational plans in order to witness the celebration of some occurrence in the life of another person unless they believed that event which brings them together to be of major importance. Almost always, such occasions are marked by some kind of ritual, and the more important the event, the more formal the ceremony. For example, in churches which teach that baptism removes original sin and confers salvation, infants are christened in traditional rites with great festivity. The infant may be dressed in a fancy, white gown which has been passed down through the family; godparents or sponsors are chosen who stand before the priest or minister with the child's parents, vowing to raise the child in the teachings of the church. Afterward a reception is often held for the family members and friends who have gathered to witness the baptism. By contrast, those churches which view baptism as a mere outward symbol of an inward conversion are more likely to baptize their people during an informal Sunday evening service or even in some church member's back yard swimming pool, with the candidate clad in shorts and a T-shirt.

By the same token, liturgical churches which teach that Christ is substantially present in the bread and wine of the communion typically surround the receiving of these elements with much more ritual than "free" or evangelical churches, which view them simply as symbols of the body and blood of the Lord. Unlike Catholics, Lutherans or Episcopalians, evangelical churches usually observe communion once a month, or even less frequently. Their communicants typically partake of the Lord's supper seated in the pew, while those in liturgical churches process to the altar, often kneeling at the rail, to be served individually by a priest or lay minister. Specific hymns are sung, traditional prayers and responses are spoken, and the entire service proceeds in accordance with the prescribed liturgy. For these churches, communion or Eucharist is the central event in the worship; hence it is observed with more ceremony.

The graduation exercises for a kindergarten class, while festive, will lack the pomp and circumstance of a high school commencement. And both of these will pale in comparison to graduation ceremonies at Annapolis or West Point.

We have pointed out that weddings are a setting for human experience within a specific cultural context. They are also an example of the way in which we confer significance upon an event through the use of ritual. Indeed, weddings are invested with what is perhaps the most elaborate of all ceremonies in our modern, Western culture. This rite of passage represents one of the most crucial steps a person takes during his or her lifetime, and the ceremony surrounding it demonstrates its importance. One's choice of a life partner affects his success, determines the ethnic makeup, personality, intelligence, social class and possibly the religion of his children, places him in a network of relationships with a new set of friends and family members, and is a major factor in the level of satisfaction he will enjoy throughout the remainder of his life. Small wonder that weddings frequently cost thousands of dollars and require months or even years of preparation. The life experiences which people take most seriously are endowed with the most extensive rituals.

The fifth function of ceremony is to provide a means for *expressing commitment*. A pledge of loyalty is intensified for the one offering it, when it is acted out in a public ritual. People do not engage in such rituals for entertainment or diversion, although they may be deeply pleasurable and satisfying. The purpose of demonstrating a commitment through a traditional, formal ceremony is to ratify and protect it. The ritual gives concrete expression to the intangible reality and makes the invisible commitment visible.

In many of the examples we have cited above, this use of ceremony is evident. At the baptism or dedication of an infant the parents typically promise to bring up the child in their faith. The wedding ceremony is an expression of a couple's devotion and of their intention to remain faithful each to the other. They could simply have their marriage license signed by witnesses and forego the expense of public celebration, but the demonstration of their pledge to one another is strengthened through the formality of the wedding. Vows taken before family and friends are not so easily set aside as those exchanged privately.

In a similar way, a person goes through an initiation ceremony to show his dedication to the organization he is about to join. Young people who approach the church altar at confirmation do so to exhibit a new relationship and commitment to the community of believers which receives them, and to the God they will worship together. They may already have made a decision within themselves to follow the Lord and even, perhaps, have verbalized it to pastor or parents, but the ritual of confirmation makes their vows visible and binding, both for themselves and for the entire congregation.

The sixth function of ceremony is to serve as a *memorial or remembrance*. Every year during the month of May we designate a Memorial Day, on which people all over the United States place flowers on the graves of loved ones, particularly those who have served in the armed forces. This annual trek to the grave side is for the purpose of remembering the life of another, and the sacrifice he made for his country.

On July fourth America recalls the war fought for its independence with thousands of processions through the streets of its cities, towns and villages. Military personnel and vehicles parade proudly among crowds of cheering spectators. Displays of fireworks are reminiscent of the bursts of gunfire exchanged during that momentous conflict, and songs about America are sung from coast to coast. The fight for our nations's independence is brought to life again on this one day each year.

On special anniversaries of the attack on Pearl Harbor or the ending of the world wars, heads of state from our own nation and others gather at the site of the events in order to remember. Bands march, speeches are given, moments of silence are observed. All of us understand the importance of memorializing these tragedies or victories which are so much a part of our nation's history.

One of the most common uses of ceremony in the act of remembering is the birthday celebration. For most of us the ritual includes a cake with candles to be blown out by the person whose birthday it is, and the receiving of presents. Wedding anniversaries have their own customs which may include the exchange of flowers or other gifts and dinner in a special restaurant.

And, of course, at the death of a loved one we gather to remember his or her life, participating in a farewell ceremony. The funeral provides a formal structure for honoring the memory of the deceased and a way of coming to terms with the fact of death. Flowers are placed on the casket, a eulogy is spoken, there is a procession to the funeral car and another to the grave site. It is a rite of memorial.

In all areas of our life, ceremony confers significance on the milestones we pass as we move from one stage to another. It says to us that these times of change and growth are important. Indeed, it intensifies their importance by calling them to our attention.

2

Ceremony
in Scripture

For Christians, who look to Holy Scriptures for guidance, it is not a sufficient validation of ceremony to show that it has always been a part of human culture. We want to know God's view of things before we commit ourselves to them. And so we turn to the sacred text to see whether our Lord approves of formality and ritual, if he perhaps forbids or abhors it, or if it is of no consequence to him at all.

We find that from Genesis to Revelation the Bible talks about ceremonies which mark significant moments in the lives of human beings. Biblical people use ceremony in a number of different contexts, some of which we will briefly discuss here.

Occasions of *celebration* have been graced with ritual from earliest times, often taking the form of dances and processions. Closely related to celebration and often overlapping it is *worship*, the observance of which is woven throughout with elaborate ritual. The ancients employed specific rites during the establishment of *covenants*, between either individuals or kingdoms. *Warfare* demanded much ceremony. *Honor* was demonstrated through its use. *Relationships* between family members often required traditional rites for their structure and functioning. And momentous events in the history of nations were *memorialized* through the use of rituals of remembrance. Examples of the use of ritual during the Biblical era are too numerous to list, but a few will be examined here to demonstrate that ceremony has always performed for God's people much the same functions it has in our own culture.

Celebration

During Old Testament times the primary rituals of celebration involved music and dancing. In most cases this was group dancing, with choreographed movements. Perhaps the first time this occurs in Scripture is at the Red Sea, after the Lord has delivered the children of Israel from bondage in Egypt. The people had witnessed a mighty miracle wrought on their behalf, which forever changed the direction of their lives and made them into a nation instead of a band of slaves. Not only so, but it was obvious that Yahweh, the God who had chosen them and formed them into a holy people, was more powerful than all the gods of Egypt put together. The appropriate response to this overwhelming reality was a ceremony of celebration, expressing the community's gratitude and its commitment to the Lord. Moses and the men of Israel sang a song of praise, which was followed by dancing with tambourines in which Miriam led the women (Exod. 15:1-21).

The writer of Judges tells the story of Jephthah the Gileadite, a man who was rejected by his fellow Israelites until they needed his strength and fighting ability to lead them in battle against the sons of Ammon. Victory for Jephthah would mean not only deliverance for his people from the threat of the Ammonites, but also a position of leadership. When he came back from defeating the enemy, his daughter celebrated with ceremony. She came out to meet her father, as the custom was for women to do following a military victory, dancing and playing her tambourine (Judg. 11:1-34). The rest of that story is too sad to tell here.

We see this same ritual occurring during the reign of King Saul in Israel. Singing, dancing and playing tambourines, the women went out to meet the armies, accompanying them as they returned to the city following the battle (1 Sam. 18:6-7).

Every year, the daughters of Shiloh participated in a festival of celebration before the Lord, in which they performed a number of dances (Judg. 21:19-21). This was apparently associated with the grape harvest, since it was carried on in the area of the vineyards.

One of the more elaborate ceremonies described in the Bible took place as King David was bringing the ark of the covenant back from Kiriath-jearim, to install it in a tent in the city of Zion. This was accomplished in two stages, since the ark was not being carried properly the first time and a second attempt had to be made. During both of them, processions of Israelites playing wind, string and percussion instruments surrounded the ark as it moved; in the second stage, David danced before the ark of the Lord "with all his might" (2 Sam. 6:14), wearing the linen ephod of a priest. In addition, when the Levites carrying the ark had gone six paces, David sacrificed animals, a ceremony in itself. The Bible relates that the whole congregation of Israel marched, shouted and played trumpets on this happy occasion (v. 15).

Covenant

A number of ceremonies adhered to the covenant process in the ancient world, and several examples of them appear in the Bible. One of the most graphic descriptions of a covenant ceremony is in Genesis 15:1-21, in which the patriarch Abram, later called Abraham, enters into covenant with Yahweh. The Lord instructs Abram to kill a heifer, a female goat, a ram, a turtledove and a young pigeon, cutting the animals in half but leaving the birds intact. These animal parts are laid out in a specified arrangement. Apparently, the usual practice was for the two parties to the covenant to walk between the parts of the slain animal as a way of identifying themselves with it. The idea was that if they broke the oath they were about to make, they could expect to come to the same end as the animals between which they were walking. Interestingly, Yahweh does not allow Abram to walk with him between the animal parts, but puts him into a deep sleep. The Lord himself moves through the pieces of the sacrifice in a double manifestation, a smoking oven and a flaming torch, so that there are still two partners involved in the ceremony. In this way the Lord takes responsibility for keeping both sides of the covenant, thereby guaranteeing its survival.

Jeremiah refers to a ceremony like this in his indictment against Israel for breaking the covenant. He writes:

> And I will give the men who have transgressed My covenant, who have not fulfilled the words of the covenant which they made before Me, when they cut the calf in two and passed between its parts . . . into the hand of their enemies (Jer. 34:18).

The implication is that the elders of Israel took part in a similar ritual to that of Abram when Yahweh made a covenant with the nation, probably at Mount Sinai (Exod. 24:10). In most cases, the covenant partners prepared and ate a meal of the sacrificed animals as part of the ceremony, often drinking its blood also. However, because the Lord had commanded his people not to consume blood, the custom in Israel was to substitute wine for the animal's blood.

The Bible relates the enactment of another covenant involving Abram, this time with the Philistine king Abimelech. There has been a dispute over water wells, and Abimelech wishes to enter into a formal peace with Abram, who is apparently a very powerful man. The stipulations are that Abram will show kindness to Abimelech and his posterity. A sacrifice and possibly a meal are implied by the fact that Abram takes sheep and oxen and gives them to Abimelech. These must have been intended for sacrifice, since Abram also sets aside seven ewe lambs as a gift for the king, to be a witness that the well has been dug by Abram and belongs to him. He then formally names the location of the well, and the oath is ratified. After Abimelech has returned home, Abram continues the ritual by planting a tamarisk tree and calling on the name of the Lord (Gen. 21:27-33).

Years later, the Lord appears to Abraham's grandson Jacob, as he flees his brother Esau's wrath and journeys toward Haran. In a dream, Jacob sees a ladder reaching to heaven, with angels ascending and descending upon it. Yahweh informs Jacob that he has been selected to inherit the covenant made with Abraham and passed down to Jacob's father Isaac. In the morning, an awe-struck Jacob performs a ritual appropriate to this noteworthy occasion. He takes the stone upon which his head rested during the encounter with the Lord, sets it up and pours oil on it. Like Abraham, Jacob names the place, and then recites a vow of faithfulness to the Lord (Gen. 28:10-21).

Much later in his life, Jacob returns to the same spot, which he has previously named Bethel ("house of God"), with flocks, herds, family and servants. The Lord has initiated this meeting and the purpose is to reaffirm his covenant with Jacob. The ceremony which ensues is similar to the earlier one. First the Lord appears to Jacob and restates the covenant promises. This time he gives to Jacob the new name Israel ("God reigns"). Jacob sets up another stone as a pillar and pours upon it both a drink offering, probably wine, and oil. Again he calls the name of the place Bethel (Gen. 35:1-15).

The covenant ceremony at mount Sinai in which Israel becomes the people of Yahweh is elaborate indeed. This is because it was through the enactment of the covenant that Israel ceased to be simply a family of former slaves and became the Lord's chosen. The covenant, with all of its ceremonies and instructions for worship, made Israel a nation. For them, then, it was the most important event of their history, and its significance was reflected in the original covenant ceremony as well as each renewal which followed. Every inch of the tabernacle and its furnishings, every garment to be worn by the priests, and every detail of the mandated sacrifices and festivals was to be executed according to the pattern given to Moses in the mountain by the Lord.

As in the covenant with Abram, the Lord himself participates in this event. First Moses calls the elders together and reads the words of the covenant to them. They respond by saying, "All that the LORD has spoken we will do" (Exod. 19:8). Next the people are consecrated and wash their clothing. On the third day the Lord appears in a cloud on the top of the mountain, occasioning thunder, flashes of lightning and the sound of a very loud trumpet. The mountain begins to quake, the trumpet grows louder, and Moses takes Aaron with him to stand before the Lord. God gives the covenant stipulations while his people stand trembling at the foot of the mountain. When he has finished, Moses repeats to the people what God has said and again they reply, "All the words which the LORD has spoken we will do" (24:23).

Moses writes down the stipulations and builds an altar at the foot of the mountain. This is not just a pile of stones, but is carefully constructed with twelve pillars to symbolize the twelve tribes of Israel. Young men offer sacrifices, and Moses collects the blood from the burnt offerings in basins, sprinkling half of it on the altar. Then he reads to the people the covenant text he has written, and they answer the third time, "All that the LORD has spoken we will do, and we will be obedient" (24:7). At this, Moses sprinkles the remaining blood on the people, saying, "Behold, the blood of the covenant, which the LORD has made with you in accordance with all these words" (24:8).

But the ceremony is not yet complete. Moses, along with Aaron and his two sons and seventy of the elders of Israel, ascend the mountain where the Bible says they actually see God and participate in a covenant meal (24:11). When they have finished eating and drinking, Moses and his servant Joshua go up into the cloud of glory on the top of the mountain, which looks to those on the ground "like a consuming fire on the mountain top" (24:17).

The book of Joshua records two instances of covenant renewal, both of which involve ceremony. In 8:30-35 we find Israel in the aftermath of the conquest of Ai. Their first attempt had been a disaster because of the sin of Achan, who had taken for himself some of the spoils of battle against the Lord's command. Here at the threshold of the promised land, Joshua renews the covenant of Yahweh with the congregation; he will be their God and they will be his people. First Joshua builds an altar of uncut stones in Mount Ebal and offers burnt offerings and peace offerings upon it. On the stones he writes Moses' law, while half the people stand before the ark of the covenant in front of Mount Gerizim and the other half stand in front of Mount Ebal, as Moses had commanded. Joshua reads "all the words of the law, the blessing and the curse . . . . before all the assembly of Israel with the women and the little ones and the strangers who were living among them" (8:34-35).

In chapter 24 we find all Israel gathered at Shechem to present themselves before the Lord. Joshua begins the renewal rite by reciting the sacred history of God's deliverance. This is followed by the taking of an oath in which Joshua offers the people a choice between Yahweh and the gods of the heathen cultures around them. Twice they respond with a vow to serve the Lord. Joshua writes the covenant in the book of the law. Then he sets up a large stone next to the sanctuary under an oak tree, designating it a witness to the covenant between Israel and Yahweh. After this the people are dismissed to return to their homes.

Both Ezra and Nehemiah officiate at a covenant renewal ceremony after the return of the exiles from Babylon to Jerusalem, as described in Nehemiah 8. The temple has been rebuilt and the city wall repaired with much effort and in spite of persecution by the Gentiles who live in the immediate area. Those Israelites who have remained in the land during the exile have corrupted themselves by intermarrying with the heathen. A renewal of the covenant with the Lord is necessary to purify and restore both the temple and the people.

Standing on a wooden platform erected for the occasion, Ezra the priest reads the law to the people assembled in the square at the Water Gate, from early morning until about noon. As he opens the book the congregation rises to its feet. He blesses the Lord and the people lift their hands toward heaven and respond, "Amen, Amen!" Then they bow themselves to the ground and worship the Lord. As Ezra reads in Hebrew, the Levites translate what he is reading into Aramaic so all can understand.

Upon hearing the commands of God and understanding how seriously they have transgressed the covenant, the great congregation begins to weep. But this is to be a joyous occasion. Ezra, along with Nehemiah the governor and the Levites admonish them to end their mourning. "Go," they tell the people, "eat of the fat, drink of the sweet, and send portions to him who has nothing prepared; for this day is holy to our Lord. Do not be grieved, for the joy of the Lord is your strength." A great festival was celebrated that day "because they understood the words which had been made known to them" (Neh. 8:10).

Biblical men also made personal covenants between individuals, which scholars refer to as "parity treaties." These, too, were fashioned according to social convention. The ritual which establishes a covenant between David and his friend Jonathan takes place in haste, in an open field, but it is nevertheless done in proper order. After the binding words are spoken in which the two men pledge loyalty to one another, Jonathan removes his robe, his armor, his bow and his weapons belt, and presents them to David (1 Sam. 18:3-4). It is common in biblical narrative to see a person share his clothing with a covenant partner, or in some cases to cover him with one's own robe, or to give him one's weapons to symbolize the treaty relationship. Examples can be found in the story of Boaz and Ruth (Ruth 3:7-9), and in the prophecies of Ezekiel (16:8), Isaiah (22:20-21), and Zechariah (3:3-5). Paul's admonition to the Ephesian Christians to wear God's armor (Eph. 6:11-17) is a reference to this custom.

The New Testament presupposes the use of ceremony in relation to the covenant, although it is not always referred to in detail. As we read through the Gospels we see that Jesus himself participated in the ceremonies appropriate to his culture. The first example is his visit to the temple in Jerusalem when he was eight days old. Luke says Jesus' parents made the journey in order to go through the ceremonies required by Jewish law (Luke 2:22-27). This included presenting him to the Lord and offering a sacrifice, as well as having the act of circumcision performed on him by the priest. The Lord himself added to the ceremony that day by sending an elderly saint named Simeon to take the Child from his parents and pronounce blessing upon him, and the aged prophetess Anna to give thanks to God for him.

At the beginning of his ministry Jesus went to the Jordan River to be baptized by John. Baptism was already a part of Jewish tradition and was performed with ceremony. Here again, the ritual was enhanced through the direct presence of God the Father. Jesus went down into the water, was baptized by John, and came up out of the water. The Holy Spirit descended upon him in the likeness of a dove, and a heavenly voice pronounced him the Son of God, or King of Israel (Matt. 3:13-17).[3]

A ceremony in which Jesus participated, and which he himself instituted and commanded, is the covenant meal or Lord's Supper. The setting was the Passover celebration which he was observing with his disciples. We will discuss later in this chapter the ritual involved in the celebration of Passover in the Old Testament. By the time Jesus and his disciples sat at table in the upper room, Passover customs had been expanded and standardized. Specifics psalms were sung, ritual prayers were said, and the meal itself followed a prescribed pattern. Near the end of this elaborate ceremony which was a renewal of the old covenant, Jesus reinterprets it in a new covenant rite. He takes bread, blesses it and gives it to his disciples, saying, "Take, eat; this is My body" (Matt. 26:26), or as Luke records it, "This is My body which is given for you; do this in remembrance of Me" (Luke 22:19). After they have eaten he passes around a cup of wine with the words, "Drink from it, all of you; for this is My blood of the covenant, which is poured out for many for forgiveness of sins" (Matt. 26:27-28).

Commenting on this ceremony, Joseph Ratzinger writes:

Assuming that the meal in question was a Passover supper, it had a fourfold structure encompassing a small preliminary meal, the Passover liturgy, the main meal, and the concluding rites. The breaking of bread took place therefore before the meal itself; the giving of the cup follows the main meal, as Luke expressly says: "*after* supper" (22:20) .... What the Lord is doing here is something new. It is woven into an old context–that of the Jewish ritual meal–but it is clearly recognizable as an independent entity. He commanded it to be

[3]J. E. Leonard, *I Will Be Their God* (Chicago: Laudemont Press, 1992), 80-81.

repeated, which implies that it was separable from the immediate context in which it took place.[4]

Ratzinger further points out that the primary element in the new covenant ceremony is the blessing of the bread and wine. That, he affirms, is the act which Jesus commanded his church to repeat. Thus the church separated out the new covenant elements from the old covenant Passover, put the blessing of the bread and cup together, and developed a distinctly Christian liturgy. As Paul expresses it:

> Is not the cup of blessing which we bless a sharing in the blood of Christ? Is not the bread which we break a sharing in the body of Christ? Since there is one bread, we who are many are one body; for we all partake of the one bread (1 Cor. 10:16-17).

Warfare

The Lord instructed Joshua to conquer Jericho by means of a ceremonial procession which went on for seven days. The Bible describes it thus:

> And the seven priests carrying the seven trumpets of rams' horns before the ark of the LORD went on continually, and blew the trumpets; and the armed men went before them, and the rear guard came after the ark of the LORD, while they continued to blow the trumpets. Thus the second day they marched around the city once and returned to the camp; they did so for six days. Then it came about on the seventh day that they rose early at the dawning of the day and marched around the city in the same manner seven times; only on that day they marched around the city seven times. And it came about at the seventh time, when the priests blew the trumpets, Joshua said to the people, "Shout! For the LORD has given you the city." . . . So the people shouted, and priests blew the trumpets; and it came about, when the people heard the sound of the trumpet, that the people shouted with a great shout and the wall fell down flat (Josh. 6:13-16, 20).

God used ritual on this occasion to effect a great victory and open the promised land to his covenant people.

A somewhat similar procession was employed by King Jehoshaphat in his battle against the sons of Ammon, Moab and Mount Seir

---

[4]Joseph Ratzinger, *The Feast of Faith* (San Francisco: Ignatius Press, 1986), 40.

who were attacking Israel. The king appointed musicians in special garments to march before the army singing praise to the Lord for his faithfulness. The enemy was routed and the army of Israel marched back to Jerusalem behind King Jehoshaphat "with harps, lyres, and trumpets to the house of the LORD" (2 Chron. 20:28).

Isaiah refers to the Lord's battle ritual in his prophecy concerning Assyria:

> For at the voice of the LORD Assyria will be terrified,
> When He strikes with the rod.
> And every blow of the rod of punishment,
> Which the LORD will lay on him,
> Will be with the music of tambourines and lyres;
> And in battles, brandishing weapons,
> He will fight them (Isa. 30:32).

Ascribing Honor

The Bible contains many examples of the use of ceremony to bestow honor upon a person or group. One is the occasion on which Joseph the Hebrew slave had correctly interpreted a dream for the Pharaoh of Egypt and the monarch wished to visibly demonstrate the esteem in which Joseph was to held by all people of the realm because of his wisdom. He did so with great solemnity. Removing his own signet ring he placed it on Joseph's hand, clothed him in robes of fine linen, and placed around his neck a gold necklace. After this he commanded that Joseph ride in procession in the Pharaoh's personal chariot with messengers running before him and crying out, "Bow the knee!" (Gen. 41:38-43).

Similarly, Mordecai the Jew was honored by King Ahasuerus for discovering a plot against the king and saving his life. Mordecai was led on horseback through the city square, dressed in the king's robe and wearing a royal crown on his head. Before him went the proclamation, "Thus it shall be done to the man whom the king desires to honor" (Est. 6:7-11).

Ceremony accompanied the process of burial in biblical times, as it does today. A description of the burial of the patriarch Jacob is given in Genesis 50:6-10. We are told that a great company of chariots, horsemen, royal servants, relatives and the elders of Egypt traveled in caravan to Canaan, where they "lamented there with a very great and sorrowful lamentation; and . . . observed seven days mourning for [Joseph's] father" (v. 10.), after which they buried him.

The kings of Judah were buried in a special place and their funerals included the building of a large fire. One exception was Manasseh, a king who had been responsible for leading the people into apostasy and bringing upon them the Lord's judgment. This exception shows that the royal burial ceremony was invested with great significance in the mind of the people–a significance thought inappropriate for an apostate king.

Relationships

A family ceremony which was common to the ancients was the blessing of children. The Bible gives at least three examples of this rite, which was usually carried out when the father perceived that he was near death. In the first example, the aged Isaac asks his oldest son Esau to go hunting for venison and make up a stew from the meat so that Isaac could eat the stew and bless his son (Gen. 27:25-29). This ceremony has covenant overtones, since it involves the killing of an animal and eating of its flesh.

In the second example, Joseph is told that his father Jacob is sick, so he takes his two young sons to receive their grandfather's blessing. The custom was to place one's right hand on the head of the older son while the blessing is being pronounced, but Jacob reverses his hands, giving the younger son the greater blessing (Gen. 48:8-22). Joseph is displeased that his father is violating the traditional form for the ritual of paternal blessing.

Later, Jacob calls his twelve sons together to bless them before he dies. Beginning with the oldest and proceeding to the youngest, Jacob pronounces a formal blessing on each one, according to their individual characters and personalities (Gen. 49:1-28).

Jesus tells the story of a son who receives his share of the inheritance from his father, and then squanders it in profligate living in a country far from home (Luke 15:11-32). When he repents and returns, the father formalizes the son's restoration to the family with a deeply significant ritual. He dresses the prodigal in the finest robe available, puts shoes on his feet, and places a signet ring, the symbol of family authority and position, on his finger. Then he instructs the servants to invite guests and prepare a feast of celebration. Receiving the young man with proper ceremony provides a social structure through which the father can express his great joy in the restoration of his son. Since the father in the story represents God, our heavenly Father, we can reasonably infer that he, too, receives back his wayward children with appropriate ceremony. Indeed, in a description of the restoration of the people of God to a new covenant relationship with Yahweh, that brought into being by Jesus Christ, the prophet Zephaniah paints a verbal picture of the utter delight the Lord takes in his restored children. Zephaniah writes:

> Do not be afraid, O Zion;
> Do not let your hands fall limp.
> The LORD your God is in your midst,
> A victorious warrior.
> He will exult over you with joy,
> He will be quiet in His love,
> He will rejoice over you with shouts of joy (Zeph. 3:16-17).

Worship

Worship without formal ceremony is unknown to biblical man. The primary act of worship beginning with Cain and Abel and continuing until the destruction of Jerusalem in AD 70, was sacrifice, which entailed elaborate ceremony. During those periods in which sacrifice was not possible such as the dispersion, or during the forty-year reign of David when the ark of the covenant resided in a tent in Zion, the Lord was worshiped with music, dancing, thanksgiving and prayer (1 Chron. 25:1-7; Pss. 149, 150). These were also ritualistic activities, sometimes involving the singing of litanies or responsive psalms (Pss. 118, 136). Consider David's description of a procession which took place in ancient Israel:

> They have seen Thy procession, O God,
> The procession of my God, my King, into the sanctuary.
> The singers went on, the musicians after them,
> In the midst of the maidens beating tambourines.
> Bless God in the congregations,
> Even the LORD, you who are of the fountain of Israel.
> There is Benjamin, the youngest, ruling them,
> The princes of Judah in their throng,
> The princes of Zebulun, the princes of Naphtali . . . .
> O God, Thou art awesome from Thy sanctuary (Ps. 68:24-27, 35).

The Lord gave detailed instructions for the ceremonies involved in setting up the tabernacle in the wilderness, even specifying the day and the month they were to take place. Each article of furniture and utensil was sanctified with anointing oil in a particular order. The lamps were lighted and the bread arranged on the table.

There were ceremonies to be carried out for the ordination of Aaron and his sons as priests. First, a basket of unleavened bread and wafers made with oil were presented to the Lord along with a bull and two rams for a sacrifice. Aaron and his sons were to wash their hands and feet at the doorway of the tent of meeting, then Moses dressed them in holy garments. After they were properly attired, anointing oil was poured over Aaron's head. The three newly robed priests were to lay their hands upon the head of the bull, and it was slaughtered. God instructed Moses to dip his finger in the animal's blood and put it on the altar before pouring the rest of the blood around the altar. Next, the priests laid their hands on the rams, which were also killed. This time Moses put the blood on the right ears, thumbs, and large toes of Aaron and his sons, pouring the rest around the altar. Portions of the sacrifice and pieces of bread were placed in Aaron's hands and then removed and waved before the Lord. The sanctuary and its furniture were touched with blood. The ritual went on and on, following the pattern given by the Lord to Moses (Exod. 29:1-46; 40:1-35).

Traditional patterns for worship are assumed in the New Testament, since the early church was part of the Jewish culture. We read about such things as Zacharias serving in the temple, Jesus being circumcised there, and the disciples going to the temple for the hour of prayer, even after the day of Pentecost when the church had become a reality. But we know very little about forms of worship in the first-century church. There is speculation as to whether Christians had a central meeting place or simply congregated in homes or various areas of the temple or elsewhere.

By the time John wrote his Revelation, however, we find a well-developed liturgy drawing much of its language and imagery from the Hebrew prophets. John himself stands in the visionary tradition of Isaiah, Ezekiel, Daniel and Zechariah as he carries a message of warning and judgment to the covenant people from the One whose countenance is as a flame of fire.

The message takes the general form of an expanded covenant lawsuit, a literary form employed by the prophets as spokesmen for the covenant when the Lord had a controversy with his people.[5] We have already noted that both the enactment and renewal of the covenant are accompanied by elaborate ceremony, and this is exactly what we find in the Revelation. In the first chapter Jesus appears as Lord of the covenant and reveals his identity. He is the Alpha and the Omega, "who is and who was and who is to come, the Almighty" (1:8). He is the One who was dead but is alive forever, and holds "the keys of death and of Hades" (v.18). In the letters to the seven churches the Lord warns his people to come out from among unbelieving Israel so that they will not share in the coming judgment.

Following the letters comes a ceremony in which the One who sits on the throne is worshiped. In front of the throne itself are seven lamps representing the seven spirits of God. Twenty-four thrones sur- round the one on which the Lord sits, and on them are elders dressed in white and wearing golden crowns. Four living creatures are also present, who do nothing but cry out, "Holy, holy, holy is the Lord God, the Almighty, who was and who is and who is to come" (Rev. 4:8). This is the signal for the elders to fall on their faces, casting their crowns before the One on the throne and responding, "Worthy art Thou, our Lord and our God, to receive glory and honor and power; for Thou didst create all things, and because of Thy will they existed, and were created" (4:11).

An angel asks for the one who is worthy to open the seals of the scroll and the Lion of the tribe of Judah is summoned. John looks and sees a Lamb who has been killed, come forward and receive the scroll. At this, the four living creatures and the twenty-four elders, each carrying a harp and holding a golden bowl full of incense, fall down before the Lamb. Together they sing to him a new song which proclaims that he is worthy to open the scroll, because through his death he has purchased a people for God "from every tribe and tongue and people and nation" (5:9). Immediately these are joined by many thousands of angels, who shout that the Lamb is worthy of all "power and riches and wisdom and might and honor and glory and blessing" (5:12).Then all creation joins the living creatures, the elders and the thousands of angels to cry, "To Him who sits on the throne, and to the Lamb, be blessing and honor and glory and dominion

---

[5]For a discussion on the structure of ancient Israelite covenants see Leonard, *I Will Be Their God.*

forever and ever" (5:13). The living creatures respond, "Amen" (5:14) and the elders fall down and worship.

After this the Lamb breaks the seals on the scroll and curses are released on those who have violated the covenant stipulations. Now appear the 144,000 followers of the Lamb who are marked with his seal on their foreheads. The 144,000 become a great multitude from all nations of the earth which cannot be counted, wearing white robes and carrying palm branches. They cry out, "Salvation to our God who sits on the throne, and to the Lamb" (7:10). Now the angels fall down before God and say, "Amen, blessing and glory and wisdom and thanksgiving and honor and power and might, be to our God forever and ever. Amen" (7:12).

Another seal is broken and an angel approaches the altar with a golden censer. He adds incense to the prayers of the saints and the mingled smoke and prayers ascend up to God. Then he fills his censer with coals from the altar and throws them to the earth, producing lightning, thunder and an earthquake. Angels sound their trumpets and plagues are released. Another angel stands with one foot on the sea and the other on the land and declares that there will be no more delay. John is given a little book and is told to eat it. Then he is commissioned to prophesy.

It is not known if the rituals John describes in his narrative were new to his readers or if they were patterned after worship as it took place in the churches to which he is writing. One authority has suggested that the structure of the Revelation to John is modeled after the Easter liturgy in its developing form.[6] In any case, it appears that certain worship practices were familiar to the congregations in the seven churches of Asia Minor. There are songs, litanies of praise, falling prostrate, and the sounding of trumpets. The wearing of holy garments, the carrying of palm branches and the burning of incense are all examples of the use of symbolism. Drama is employed in the actions of the angels. Here is a form of worship associated with the New Testament church which is highly symbolic and ceremonial in character.

---

[6]Massey H. Shepherd, Jr., *The Paschal Liturgy and the Apocalypse* (Richmond, Virginia: John Knox Press, 1960), 77.

Memorial

In addition to the tabernacle worship, Yahweh instituted three annual feasts which Israel was to celebrate. All three were related in some way to the deliverance from Egyptian bondage which made Israel a nation and brought it into covenant with Yahweh. Each feast had its own special ceremonies, depending upon the particular aspect of the Exodus event which was being memorialized.

Passover recalled the night when God's angel of death visited all the households of Egypt, but passed over the dwellings of Israel which had the blood of a slain lamb splashed on their doorpost and lintel (Deut. 16:1-3). Seven days of eating no bread containing leaven preceded Passover, and the day itself was observed with a special meal. The first Passover meal was eaten in haste, with loins girded, sandals on the feet and staff in hand (Exod. 12:11). Whether these instructions apply to the annual feast is not clear. In any case the menu consisted of an unblemished, one-year-old lamb, sacrificed at sunset (Deut. 16:6), along with unleavened bread and bitter herbs (vv. 3-8). A solemn assembly took place on the final day of the feast (16:8).

Fifty days after Passover was the time established for the Feast of Weeks or Pentecost. This was an occasion for rejoicing, in which the people were to remember that they were once slaves in Egypt (Deut. 16:10-12), but were now established in the promised land, enjoying its bounty. At Pentecost Israel brought a free-will offering of the first fruits of the wheat harvest (Exod. 34:22) in thanksgiving for the blessings of the Lord.

The third of the great memorial celebrations was the Feast of Booths or Tabernacles. This was also a harvest festival, observed after the grain and grape harvests were completed. During this feast the people were commanded to rejoice exceedingly. Remembering the forty-year trek through the wilderness when Israel resided in temporary shelters, they were to live in arbors or tabernacles made of tree branches for seven days (Lev. 23:39-43; Deut. 16:13-15).

Jesus said that the covenant meal or Eucharist is a memorial to his death. This is not for the purpose of remembering the pain and suffering he bore for the sake of mankind, but a reminder of what that sacrifice accomplished. As Christians join in receiving the bread and wine of the holy meal, they do so as the very body of the Lord, the new man or new creation which he died to initiate. Feasting on his body and blood, they identify with Christ's death to the old covenant and his initiation of the new. Thus they celebrate the Passover meal of the new covenant, the great deliverance wrought by God on behalf of his people.

Conclusion

The biblical record clearly demonstrates that the human penchant for ceremony is a gift from God. Not only does he create rituals for his people to observe, but the Lord often breaks into the human scene to add to or enhance rituals already in existence. The only conclusion one can draw from this evidence is that the Creator has placed in human beings a desire for dignifying significant events with ceremony, and that such ceremony has his blessing. In fact, it can be argued that the Lord *commands* the use of ritual.

3

Worship: Cognitive or Symbolic?

Since the Bible is full of ceremony and ritual, why is it that so many evangelical Christians seem to fear formal structure and ceremony in the church? Surely, if we looked to the Scriptures as a pattern, as virtually all evangelical and charismatic churches claim to do, our worship would be radically different from what it is. What has initiated and perpetuated the myth that ritual is somehow unspiritual, and that worship has to be completely unstructured or spontaneous in order to be acceptable to God?

Not only are we of the "free" tradition wary of ceremony; we also disdain the use of symbols. Such things as stained glass windows depicting Bible characters, or the use of the cross, dove, triangle, the loaf and chalice, or other representations of the Christian faith are avoided as being akin to idolatry. But a survey of the divine directions for building the tabernacle, and later the temple, should lay to rest such notions. The mighty cherubim which overshadow the ark of the covenant are of beaten gold, the work of a gifted artisan. So, too, is the lampstand with its cloud of fragrant incense which mingles with the scent of fresh bread from the golden table, drifting out into the courtyard where it spirals upward in the smoke from the bronze altar. Brilliant white curtains surround the entire enclosure, richly embroidered with figures of trees, flowers and cherubs. Priests go about their assigned tasks, resplendent in specially decorated robes.

Everywhere we turn, we find color, texture, shimmer, sweet odors and religious symbol.

Evelyn Underhill, writing in the 1930s, explains that ritual and symbol are important to Christian worship because both our physical and spiritual natures must be offered to God. Worship, she says, has historically included four basic components: ritual, symbol, sacrament and sacrifice. Like the human person, these also have

> a visible action and an invisible action, both real, both needed, and so closely interdependent that each loses its true quality if torn apart; for indeed an idolatry which pins religion to abstract thoughts and notions alone is not much better than an idolatry which pins it to concrete stocks and stones alone. Either of these extremes are impoverishments.[7]

God has revealed himself to us in ways which touch both our inner natures and our physical senses in Jesus Christ, the fully human expression of the invisible God. We, in turn, respond to him most effectively "not by a simple movement of the mind; but by a rich and complex action, in which [our] whole nature is concerned."[8] Humans are made to combine "thought and speech . . . gesture and manual action" and when we worship we must use them all if our offering is to engage our whole being. "Religious action," says Underhill,

> must be social, as well as personal; rhythmic and ceremonial, as well as interior and free . . . .so that the whole of [a person's] nature plays its part in his total response to the Unseen.[9]

She quotes W. H. Frere as follows:

> It is a form of blindness, not common sense, that prevents a man from recognizing that behind ceremonies there lie realities–principles, doctrines, and states or habits of mind. No one can hope to judge fairly of matters of ceremonial who does not see that the reason why they cause such heat of controversy is that they signify so much.[10]

---

[7]Evelyn Underhill, *Worship* (New York: Harper & Brothers, 1936), 23.

[8]Ibid.

[9]Ibid.

[10]W. H. Frere, *The Principles of Religious Ceremonial*, 9, as quoted in Underhill, 23.

Thomas Howard, himself a former evangelical, writes thus about the importance of symbolism:

> It is in the physical world that the intangible meets us. A kiss seals a courtship. The sexual act seals a marriage. A ring betokens the marriage. A diploma crowns years of schooling. A doctoral robe bespeaks intellectual achievement. A uniform and stripes announce a recruit's training. A crown girds the brow that rules England. This symbolism bespeaks the sort of creature we are. To excise all of this from piety and worship is to suggest that the gospel beckons us away from our humanity into a disembodied realm. It is to turn the Incarnation into a mere doctrine.[11]

In *The Shape of the Liturgy*, Gregory Dix explains the essential difference between the two major theories of worship: the intellectual model which emphasizes cognitive acceptance of salvation principles in an internal contract with God, and the liturgical model, which stresses the involvement of the whole person in the process of receiving and acting out one's salvation. He writes:

> Briefly, the puritan theory is that worship is a purely mental activity, to be exercised by a strictly psychological "attention" to a subjective emotional or spiritual experience . . . . Over against this puritan theory of worship stands another–the "ceremonious" conception of worship, whose foundation principle is that worship as such is not a purely intellectual and affective exercise, but one in which the whole man–body as well as soul, his aesthetic and volitional as well as his intellectual powers–must take full part. It regards worship as an "act" just as much as an "experience."[12]

As far as worship itself is concerned, biblical man knew nothing about a private faith. The covenant with Yahweh was a corporate treaty, involving all members of the community, and all of them participated in open, visible, physical, ceremonial worship. We must admit that this is not the case in many of our evangelical churches today. Salvation is too often thought of in terms of an internal contract between God and the individual. We are cautioned not to

---

[11]Thomas Howard, *Evangelical is Not Enough* (San Francisco: Ignatius Press, 1984), 36.

[12]Gregory Dix, *The Shape of the Liturgy* (New York: Seabury Press, [1945] 1983), 312.

judge a professed believer's commitment to the Lord by whether or not he or she appears to be involved in worship or any other external behavior, since "only God knows the heart." Faith is said to be a matter between the person and God and is the business of no one else.

In fact, members in many churches would be scandalized or at least embarrassed were some person to openly demonstrate devotion or to be visibly moved by an encounter with the Lord in the sphere of public worship. Let a worshiper kneel, lift the hands, begin to weep or perhaps to dance, and the ushers might very well quietly escort him or her out of the sanctuary. "Decently and in order" has come to mean emotionless, colorless, and above all, quiet.

Why is this so? One must ask whether evangelicals have distanced themselves from ceremony and other biblical forms of praise to God because they are avoiding expression of a visible commitment. After all, the assent to faith or vow to godliness which supposedly takes place in "the heart" and is not externally apparent, can be forgotten or discarded without anyone's being the wiser. Such internal commitment is often no commitment at all. Thomas Howard comments:

> To restrict . . . worship to sitting in pews and listening to words spoken is to narrow things down in a manner strange to the gospel. We are creatures who are made to bow, not just spiritually (angels can do that) but with kneebones and neck muscles. We are creatures who cry out to surge in great procession, "*ad altare Dei*," not just in our hearts (disembodied spirits can do that) but with our feet, singing great hymns with our tongues, our nostrils full of the smoke of incense.[13]

If this is thought to be "too physical," Howard continues, then we must do away with all of the physical aspects of the gospel story including "the stable and the manger, and the winepots at Cana, and the tired feet anointed with nard, and the splinters of the cross, not to say the womb of the mother who bore God when he came to us."[14]

If demonstrative worship is thought to be too emotional, we must ask ourselves if our emotions are not also a part of God's good creation, given to us so that we will be *able* to respond to him. To

---

[13]Ibid., 37.

[14]Ibid.

relegate religious experience to the intellectual and spiritual while denying the physical and emotional any share in our faith is to create an artificial dichotomy and is, in fact, a form of Gnosticism. It gives substance to the heretical idea that the body is somehow evil and only the internal, spiritual part of the person is acceptable to God. St. Paul instructs us to the contrary when he admonishes the Christians in Rome to present their entire bodies as sacrifices to God (Rom. 12:1), and tells the Philippians to rejoice (Phil. 4:4). Clearly there are physical and emotional actions in which we can engage that glorify God and enrich our relationship with him.

It can be argued that expressing our love for God in a visible action actually increases that devotion. Howard reflects on the effect of our actions upon our inner motivation thus:

> We renounce the divided world where body wars against heart and where gesture struggles with thought. By enacting what is true, we learn what is true. By bowing with our heads as well as our hearts, we testify to the restored seamlessness of outer and inner. By bowing with the knee we teach our reluctant hearts to bow. By making the sign of the cross with our hands we signal to heaven, earth, hell, and to our own innermost beings that we are indeed under this sign–that we are crucified with Christ. No longer do we refuse the outer gesture in the name of the inner faith. Buddhism, Platonism, and Manichaeanism may do so, but Christian faith cries out to be shaped.[15]

Ceremony is part of the process by which our Christian commitment is given shape and expression. The use of ceremony and symbol deserves greater attention than it has received in many Christian congregations.

---

[15]Ibid., 104.

4

A Walk Through History

If God has made us to worship him with all of our being, what has happened to convince us that exuberant, expressive or ceremonial worship is to be avoided? There may be many answers to that question. However, a look at some of the events of religious history may help us understand in part how we have developed antipathy toward religious ceremony and symbol.

To begin with, Christian tradition began to undergo a profound change after Christianity became the state religion under the Roman emperor Constantine in the early part of the fourth century. Not all citizens of the empire, made up of peoples who had been steeped in polytheism for centuries, were ready to give up the worship of their pagan idols simply because the existing government decreed that they had been converted and were now to worship God through his Son Jesus Christ. Moreover, invading Germanic tribes were assimilated into the empire and so into the church, bringing with them additional heathen traditions.

Pagan religions included popular community festivals, many of which were related to the seasonal cycle and as such employed fertility rites as a part of worship. These were not customs the superstitious peasants wanted to relinquish. So it was that the church, which was now headquartered in the capital city of Rome, employed synthesis to solve the religious problem.

A major deity in all ancient religions was the sun god Ba'al, who was known by various names, depending upon one's particular culture and language. According to legend, Ba'al's wife Ishtar, (also known as Astarte or Ashtoreth) bore him a son named Tammuz. The worship of the goddess and her child was an important part of nearly all pagan religious systems, and the Bible makes a number of references to this practice. If the people of the Roman Empire could not be persuaded to abandon shrines dedicated to Ishtar and Tammuz and the gods which had become part of the Roman pantheon in order to worship a God they could not see, then the reasonable thing to do was to convert the shrines rather than the people. Ishtar might easily become the Virgin Mary, with Tammuz transformed into the infant Jesus. Other idols could be renamed for Christian figures such as apostles or other saints. Surely it would be preferable for the intractable pagans to venerate persons associated with Christianity than to be bowing to symbols of demonic gods which the shrines had originally represented.[16]

Especially dear to the hearts of the people was the traditional winter festival celebrating the birthday of Tammuz at the winter solstice on December 25, when the sun began to return northward. As a witness to the gospel, the church instituted a Christian feast on the same day, in which it celebrated the birth of Jesus Christ. Inevitably, over a period of time many of the pagan customs found their way into the Christian festival. The use of wreaths, the hanging of shiny balls to represent the sun, decorating with holly and ivy, and many of our Christmas customs originated in this ancient winter festival.

While the pagans observed a period of mourning for Tammuz between his "death" each winter and his subsequent "resurrection" each spring, the church commemorated Christ's forty days under assault by the devil in the wilderness. And whereas the period of mourning for Tammuz erupted into a spring festival which celebrated the pagan sun god, Christians ended their forty-day Lenten period with a joyous proclamation of the resurrection of the Son of God. Here, again, synthesis occurred over the centuries. Fertility symbols associated with the old feast such as eggs, spring bulbs and baby rabbits became symbols of new life in Jesus. The day of resurrection began to be called by the name of the goddess Ishtar, or "Easter." Many of the peasants still looked to the saints as gods;

---

[16]Ralph Woodrow, *Babylon Mystery Religion* (Riverside, California: Ralph Woodrow Evangelistic Association, 1966), 13-20, 30-38.

miracles were attributed to them and to them were directed prayers and homage.[17] The church was not unduly alarmed. It has historically accommodated itself to the local customs of evangelized tribes, wherever possible, believing that when these practices are dedicated to the worship of God they lose their original purpose and take on Christian significance.

The task of instructing new converts to Christianity was overwhelming to the point of impossibility, particularly because most of the peasants and even some of the priests were illiterate. At various times schools were established for the purpose of teaching both adults and children to read. The church employed architecture, drama and other art forms such as stained glass windows, sculptures and paintings to educate its people. During some periods these methods were effective while at other times they proved inadequate. Superstition and pagan practices persisted, leading to the development and proliferation of popular beliefs which included elements of magic and idolatry held over from the old religions.

There was also the problem of secularization. When a religion is adopted as the official faith of the state, it is almost inevitable that it will eventually become politicized and thereby corrupted. Christianity was no exception, and over the centuries it saw the degeneration of both its moral standards and teachings. True devotion to Christ and understanding of the faith were often relegated to the convent or monastery, while clerical positions were political appointments rather than an affirmation of a person's spiritual calling.[18] It became common practice for church leaders to take advantage of the ignorance of the laity, promising forgiveness and absolution in return for the payment of money. The once vibrant, life-changing faith bore little resemblance to the apostolic witness of the Scriptures. It was against this corruption that the Protestant reformers protested with understandable outrage.

Men like Martin Luther and Philipp Melanchthon in Germany, John Calvin and Huldreich Zwingli in Switzerland, John Knox in Scotland and others like them, also took issue with Catholic doctrines. They insisted that the Bible be made available to people of all classes,

---

[17]Ibid., 143-152.

[18]Edward Rice, *The Church: A Pictorial History* (New York: Farrar, Straus & Cudahy, 1961), 96.

whereas the Church had withheld the Scriptures from the laity, fearing misinterpretation and heresy. They opposed the sale of indulgences, taught that a person is saved by faith alone and that the sacraments were not necessary to attain a state of grace.

At first the conflict between the Church and the dissenters took the form of debate and oratory. The invention and widespread use of the printing press and the block print made it possible for both sides to print their arguments and distribute them, many embellished with cartoons and other illustrations. But eventually the war of words erupted into a war of weapons in which churches were destroyed and many on both sides were imprisoned or killed. The Catholic Church attempted to reform itself, but the changes came too late. Christianity had become deeply divided.

The Reformation in England did not begin over either corruption or matters of doctrine, but was the result of King Henry VIII's desire to divorce his wife and marry his mistress. Henry did not actually leave the Catholic church but merely declared himself to be its head in England. Thus the English or Anglican church was not Protestant in the same sense as the Reformed and Lutheran movements in Europe, and it retained many of the practices and teachings of the Roman Catholics.

During the fifteenth and sixteenth centuries, however, opposition arose against the established church, manifesting itself in the proliferation of small groups of protesters, or Protestants, who met in homes or other private places to worship God in simplicity. Their meetings were largely devoid of ceremony, and the meeting places without symbol, as a reaction against the more elaborate liturgy of the Anglo-Catholics. Worship was typically spontaneous, unstructured and enthusiastic. The government forbade such meetings, which they called "conventicles,"[19] and those separatists who persisted in gathering for worship not authorized by the state church were persecuted and even imprisoned. In 1600 some of them fled to Holland.

Eventually the whole conflict became political, with Oliver Cromwell, leader of the Separatist or Congregational movement pitted against Charles, head of the state church, and his Anglican Royalists. After a series of maneuverings and a civil war, Cromwell

---

[19]James Harvey Robinson, *Medieval and Modern Times* (Boston: Ginn and Company, 1902), 372.

succeeded in overthrowing Charles and had him beheaded for treason in 1649, himself becoming Lord Protector of England.[20] Under Cromwell's leadership strict moral practices were introduced into the army, statues and symbols were removed from all churches, and the possession or practice of anything "popish" such as the celebration of Christmas and other Catholic observances was cause for punishment.[21]

After the death of Cromwell in 1658, the Royalists were reinstated under Charles II. Once again Separatists began to be persecuted. The Conventicle Act was passed, forbidding Separatist meetings, which were viewed as rebellion against the state church, hence the Crown.[22] Many separatists migrated to the new world, establishing Congregational churches in the American colonies. The first of these were the group we know today as the Pilgrims, whose faith and fortitude are celebrated in late November all over America during the festival we call Thanksgiving.

Feelings of bitterness toward their Anglican Catholic persecutors continued to run high among the colonists and their worship practices gave evidence of their aversion to anything connected with that hated religion. Meeting houses were plain and unadorned. Each church was autonomous, governing itself without interference from any hierarchy. Ceremony and ritual were avoided. Congregationalism became the established religion of the Massachusetts Bay Colony and Connecticut. The New England Congregationalists founded Harvard and Yale Colleges for the purpose of training ministers. Thus, from the beginning, American Protestant faith was essentially a protest against the decadence and corruption which had for centuries characterized the Roman and Anglican churches. It is this Separatist, Congregationalist foundation which has infused into American culture a strongly independent individualism. And while this individualism has its values, it also tends to diminish our sense of community, heritage and tradition.

---

[20]Ibid., 376.

[21]Elizabeth Goudge, *The Child From the Sea* (New York: Coward-McCann, Inc., 1970), 316-317.

[22]Ibid., 383.

5

The Problem of Individualism

The protest against Catholicism, then, is not the only factor in the repudiation of symbol and ceremony in American evangelical Christianity. Individualism became enculturated in the Separatist movement and a high value was placed upon it. But such a philosophy militates against the exercise of ritual which requires participation by the entire group in one corporate expression of faith. Tradition belongs to the community, and ceremony is the means by which it expresses itself. To engage in ceremony is to commit oneself to the tradition of the community; one does not engage in it privately and alone.

The idea of independence is woven into the very fabric of this country, whose people were willing to give their lives for it when the nation was founded. Traditionally, Americans have placed a higher value upon our independence than upon our relationship to the community. Understandably, then, participation in the traditions of group culture can be threatening to us.

But individualism is not the way of Christianity, as it is defined in the Bible. The Scriptures declare that Jesus Christ came to establish a holy *people*. He died for the *church*. Christianity means accepting membership in a *kingdom* and becoming part of an *army*, which involves marching in group formation. Christians together are the *body* of Christ. And the new covenant mandates relationship with one's *brothers and sisters* as well as with the covenant Lord. All of

51

these images are corporate—there is no place found for the individual Christian who refuses to be connected to the community of saints.

As we have observed, a lack of ceremony is not confined to the church alone. The unprecedented mobility of this generation has contributed to our sense of individuality by making people anonymous and therefore less obligated to society or inclined toward maintaining standards and mores of the culture. If those a person meets in the store, on the street or even in the neighborhood do not recognize him or know his name, he will not be unduly concerned about either his appearance or his actions. And there is a trend toward tolerance in all areas of life which lessens the threat of anyone's being judged on the basis of his behavior.

Perhaps it is this very mobility which has produced in many Christians a sense of isolation. The loss of extended family structures and the tenuous nature of our relationships has made us aware of the need to be connected to the body and touched by the transcendent. These longings cannot be assuaged by a casual approach to religion. And there can be no mistaking the fact that a significant number of Bible-believing Christians recognize the void in their lives and have begun a move back to the liturgical church. Several well-known Protestant pastors have given up their highly effective ministries to become Roman Catholic laymen. Episcopal churches surrounding a prestigious Midwestern evangelical college are filling up with students who are dissatisfied with their experience of the spiritual. Entire evangelical and charismatic churches are petitioning to join liturgical denominations. New denominations are being formed which combine an evangelical commitment to the Scriptures with the practice of historic Christian liturgy.

A recent study of these phenomena shows that many, if not most, of those who are making this change are lifelong evangelicals. Many have graduated from Bible institutes or colleges. They are choosing the liturgical church not because their love for the Lord has cooled, but because they seek a more meaningful relationship with him. If you ask them why they are doing this, they will tell you that they hunger for a more intense experience of the majesty and mystery of God in worship. They want to be connected with the historical church which has carried the banner of faith throughout history, and which now extends across the world. And they seek a sense of the immediate presence of the Lord in the communion service, and more frequent observance of the holy meal. Respondents to a questionnaire distributed to a group of these former evangelicals say they derive both a feeling of awe and a sense of community through participation in the liturgy, which is essentially sacred ritual.[23]

The research seems to indicate that there is a growing desire in evangelical circles for the use of ceremony which will ascribe significance to worship, link worshipers to the community of believers, and allow them to express commitment in a visible way. It is an intense hunger, to cause those who experience it to abandon church affiliations which may span a lifetime. In some cases it has caused ruptures in families and among friends. Not all Christians are brave enough to risk the change, but this does not mean that many of them do not sense the same stirrings within themselves for a more intense and communal expression of worship although they may be reluctant to verbalize the need. Perhaps the evangelical church should take a hard look at what respondents to the questionnaire describe as "sterile" worship in many of their former congregations. The inclusion of biblical patterns of ceremony might help more of its parishioners to find satisfaction in a richer and more expressive encounter with God.

It is significant that in the armed forces of the United States, where group cohesiveness is sometimes crucial to survival, the casual approach is not in vogue. Virtually everything that is done in a military setting is accompanied by rigid protocol and prescribed ceremony, regardless of circumstances. Even in the wilds, far from civilization, or surrounded by the chaos of battle, proper ritual is observed. The result is a military organization whose members are committed and loyal, not only to their own particular branch of the armed services but to the country as a whole.

If in this modern, uncommitted, casual age our military forces can successfully maintain ceremoniousness to their distinct advantage, can it be truthfully said that the church is not able to do the same? And especially so, since it is part of the pattern given to us by our Lord? If those who serve their country in the military services are not embarrassed by an externally expressed loyalty to one another and to their leadership, neither should we who serve the living God and are members of the community of faith be embarrassed by acts of

---

[23]Research project by the author for a course of study at Trinity College, Deerfield, Illinois, 1992.

devotion to him and to one another. Indeed, we might rather create new and exciting ways in which we can demonstrate our fidelity to the kingdom of God and our identity within it.

6

Renewing Our Worship

Now that we have begun to understand the usefulness and desirability of ritual in celebrating our Christian faith, we must discover how we can bring it into the average evangelical church. Each church is distinctive in its theological perspective, its history and tradition, and in the atmosphere and personality which characterize it. We do not wish to offend those faithful people who come to our churches because they are comfortable with the style of worship there. But neither do we want to leave them unfulfilled or to provide less than a complete experience of the presence of God in our midst. Where does a local church begin to modify its customs in order to incorporate appropriate ceremony? And how does it know what is and what is not appropriate?

From all that we read in Scripture, we know that pastors are responsible to impart truth to their people. Developing festive and ceremonial worship is a task for the church leadership and will only be accomplished if they are fully committed to it. Some have made the mistake of expecting worship to occur spontaneously in the congregation, leaving the process entirely to the Holy Spirit. But this overlooks the leadership role which is incumbent upon those whom the Lord has placed in charge of the flock. Seldom will the Lord introduce the renewal of worship into a congregation whose pastor is intent on defending the status quo.

Basically, a church can be introduced to a new style of worship in two ways. The first of these is instruction. Before ceremony can successfully be integrated into the worship of an evangelical church, the people must be taught concerning its importance and meaning. Once they fully understand that the Lord approves of ritual and symbol, and that their use will bring him glory, they will be able to accept and be enriched by them.

Second, the church staff must model the new behavior, becoming personally involved in expressive worship. No worshiper has permission to participate in an external demonstration of faith until he sees those in leadership do so. They grant him or her that permission by setting the example. If the pastor is unwilling to engage in visual acts of devotion, neither will the congregation be able to do so. But the leaders who give themselves fully to worship in full view of the laity will find it easier to bring their people along with them into a more complete expression of devotion to God.

There are a number of ways in which an evangelical church can enhance its worship with ritual and symbol. We can begin with the rite which Jesus himself instituted, which lies at the very heart of the Christian faith, the Lord's Supper. To begin, we can stop treating it in a casual or routine manner, tacking it onto the end of the church service as if it were an afterthought. The early church understood the Eucharist to be a holy and vital communion with the Lord. Those of the group who had not been received into the community by baptism were not permitted even to view the rite. This was the renewal of the new covenant, a participation in the body and blood of the Savior. Therefore it was entered into with much solemnity. In our churches, too, we can acknowledge the importance of this event by enduing it with reverent ceremony.

Communion is a gathering together into one, the renewing of the mutual faith of the covenant people. It was never meant to be a time of private devotion between the Lord and the individual Christian. We can demonstrate the community aspect of the Supper by the way in which we observe it. When we serve worshipers privately as they sit in the pew, asking them to personally inspect the condition of their souls, we are reinforcing individualism. But if we ask people to come forward together to receive the bread and wine at the Lord's Table, we create an occasion for ceremony and for a public expression of faith. In so doing, we turn the observance of the Lord's Supper into the community celebration of the new covenant which it was intended to be.

Of course it is important to confess sin before participating in the holy meal. But St. Paul's admonition to examine oneself before eating and drinking, found in 1 Corinthians 11:28, is a warning about discerning the *body*. That is, he was concerned that those who ate and drank were mindful of their relationship to one another in the family of God. He was not asking the Corinthians to examine their inner motives or search for some hidden transgression they needed to confess. Ruptures among believers in the community are the offenses being discussed here. It is, after all, the sacrifice of our Lord this ceremony represents which makes the believer worthy to participate in the covenant meal–not his or her state of sinlessness.

The Lord's Supper is a time for rejoicing in the fact of the new covenant and the existence of this people for whose creation Jesus gave his life. Those who were not a people are now the people of God (1 Pet. 2:10). Eminently suitable for this occasion, then, are corporate prayers, corporate singing and corporate responses.[24]

Another occasion for holy ceremony in the evangelical church is the dedication of infants. The use of meaningful ritual on these occasions can enhance the joy experienced by the parents and relatives of the children. It can also signify to them and to the whole church the importance of the vows being taken to bring up these little ones in the fear and love of God.

Instead of impersonal, mass productions, in which the pastor prays a generic prayer over ten or twelve infants in the arms of anonymous parents, this important act of giving a new human life back to God can be made memorable. The ritual should recognize each child as an individual, welcoming him or her by name into the community of faith. The gathered church should also be asked to commit itself to the family, to assist in the task of rearing the child in the faith by modeling Christianity before him or her, and to nurture the child in the love of Jesus. These reciprocal vows, taken by both parents and congregation, effectively connect both the infant and his family to the body of Christ.

---

[24]Some excellent resources for developing a liturgy of communion can be found in Robert E. Webber, ed., *The Complete Library of Christian Worship* (Nashville: Abbott Martyn Press, 1994).

On this subject, it might be well for evangelical Christians to note that according to Paul's letter to the Colossians baptism is the new covenant equivalent of old covenant circumcision (2:11-12). In obedience to God's directions, Israelite and Jewish babies were circumcised under the Mosaic law at the age of eight days, long before they were capable of making a personal, rational commitment to the ways of the Lord. If baptism, like circumcision, is a sign of entrance into the covenant community, perhaps it is, after all, appropriate for children.

But whether or not one can accept the baptism of infants, the liturgical practice of confirmation for children who have attained the age of reason is one that evangelical congregations might profitably emulate. This is another opportunity to affirm a child in the faith or to bring him or her to a point of personal acceptance of Christ as Savior. The practice of confirmation allows the pastor or other church leader to have a personal impact on the church children and to build relationships with them which may be vitally important as they mature and encounter the inevitable doubts.

Formal instruction in the Christian faith is given in a series of classes, and is climaxed by a time in which each participant is asked to personally accept it for himself. The commitments thus made are celebrated in a public ceremony before the entire church, which might include anointing with oil, or for those who are newly converted, baptism. Especially meaningful at this time is a sealing of the commitment to the community of faith by participation in the Eucharist with the whole church. The class might then be received into the church fellowship by means of a ritual of questions and responses in which the congregation participates.

This kind of public ceremony confers significance upon the rite of passage it celebrates. It elevates to importance the effort and diligence each child has invested in preparation for church membership. Through the act of the congregation it pronounces God's blessing on the child's life. It creates a sense of brotherhood among the confirmands. And it binds the children together with the rest of the worshiping body. Children who are lovingly nurtured through this process by adult Christians who obviously care about them are more apt to take seriously their relationship to their church because the church is demonstrating that it takes the child seriously. The entire religious community should pause to mark each important step in a person's spiritual life, thereby conferring significance upon it.

We have mentioned the celebration of contemporary events in the life of the church family as occasions which may be enhanced by the use of ritual and symbol. But the commemoration of key events in the history of our faith also offers rich opportunities to adapt patterns of festive worship which are found in the Pentateuch, the Psalms and the Revelation to John for use in the church. Processions, perhaps with banners, to initiate the worship on these special days can project a sense of God's majesty and glory. Candles may be lit and carried to symbolize the Light which is Christ in our midst. The liturgy might include spoken or sung litanies in which the congregation responds to the leader in a commitment to faith. Scripture passages read responsively serve to proclaim the Word of God while creating the cohesiveness of community. Christmas and Easter celebrations can effectively make use of appropriate floral offerings, which not only delight the eye but exude a glorious fragrance as well. Pentecost Sunday might feature a liturgical dance to symbolize the tongues of fire and rushing wind experienced by the first church as it gathered in the upper room.

Paul tells us that the Lord has ordained that his children should do good works (Eph. 2:10). He draws a verbal picture of the usefulness of each member of the body as he or she uses the gifts God has given to grace the community (1 Cor. 12:12-30). We in local congregations need to identify those special people of creativity and imagination whom God has placed in our midst, and then free them to discover new ways in which we can glorify our great King through our worship. As they exercise their gifts both they and the church will be blessed.

7

ConcLusion

Let us never forget that Luther, Calvin, Knox and the other Protestant reformers opposed the Roman Catholic Church because of moral corruption among the clergy and bishops, the practice of selling indulgences, and the failure to make the Bible accessible to the laity. They were not opposed to the ritual and symbolism of the church liturgy. These were abandoned by adherents of the "free" church movement in a general repudiation of anything that "looks Catholic." Even the reception of Holy Communion was somewhat suspect, and the frequency of its observance was drastically curtailed. How we have impoverished ourselves in our attempts to establish our own identity!

It is now time for the evangelical church to stop rejecting ceremony and symbol in an outdated protest against the abuses of centuries past. If we are honest we will admit that our own Protestant forefathers were not without fault in their treatment of those with whom they disagreed. Surely the Lord was grieved over the slaughter of both Catholics and Protestants which was carried out in his name. None of us has a religious heritage free of stain and embarrassment. All branches of the Christian faith have gone through periods of apostasy and have struggled with heresy and abuses of power.

Protestant Christians are indebted to the historic church for its preservation of the Holy Scriptures and for guarding the Christian faith since the time of the apostles. The Spirit of God did not abandon the church because it went through times of corruption and spiritual decline; when it went off course he brought reform and renewal to bring it back. The Reformation itself was a part of that process.

Our purpose as Christians is not to make philosophical statements about who we are. Rather, it is to bring homage and adoration to the Lord our God with as full an expression of devotion as we can produce. We have seen that ritual and symbol are gifts from God which infuse our lives with meaning and our worship with depth. Therefore, let us embrace them and give thanks.

We are the people of God, the community of faith, the army of the Lord. As one body, then, let us lift high his banners and make his praise glorious, marching together in the age-old *processions of God*.